WHEN OPPORTUNITY KNOCKS

Cheri Schultz

When Opportunity Knocks

For information on quantity discounts, please write to:
Cheri A Schultz
10536 Jayne Valley Ln
Fenton, MI 48430-USA

Published by:
ECS Enterprises
10536 Jayne Valley Ln
Fenton, MI 48430-USA

Acknowledgements

To God who makes all things possible. You gave me strength and faith to pursue my dreams and now they have become my reality. Glory and honor to you Almighty Father.

To Eric, my husband, who is my rock, strength and confidant. Without his support, love and guidance, I could have never climbed this mountain. He has always encouraged me to believe in myself and gave me the confidence to keep moving forward. I love you forever more.

To Laura, my sister, my best friend. Whenever I needed a listening ear or shoulder to cry on, she welcomed me with open arms. Her warmth and strength help me endure when the burden was great. I am forever grateful.

To my Family, whose constant support and love gave me hope and strength. Thank you for always being my prayer warriors.

To my Spiritual Coach, Kailo, who has inspired me to dream large. I will be forever changed by her compassion, honesty, love and kind words.

Prologue

At approximately 8 pm my cell phone rings; it's my nephew and he sounds out of breath. Hi Aunt Cheri, this is Will, I am in need of two, one liter pop bottles. Do you have any? I said yes, c'mon over. My nephew lives two doors down.

Within minutes the doorbell rings and in races Will with his pajama bottoms and a pair of shoes two sizes too big. I said it's pretty late, "What are you working on?" He said, "I need to build two Rocket Ships tonight and study for my Science final." I said "It sounds like you have a lot on your plate". He replies "Yes, you're probably right but when I realized how much I had to study, I think I may only get a "B", so I am building these rockets to get some extra credit. You see if I build these Rocket Ships and they go the furthest, I can get extra points added to my final exam."

I said, "Let's just back up a minute. What makes you think you won't be getting an "A" on this test tomorrow." Oh Aunt Cheri, it's going to be really hard and I don't think I can." I said "Okay, let me help you achieve this "A" and overcome your fear by doing a little exercise. I said, "Every time you ***THINK*** you're going to get a "B", change it to: I am capable, I am smart and I have studied all the information I need to get an "A" on the test. Is that fair"? He said, "Okay, Aunt Cheri I will try this exercise when I feel anxious about the "B", but I have to go because I have to study and build my Rocket Ships." I kissed and hugged him as he left, and as he was walking down the sidewalk, I yelled out his name. I said, "Will what are you going to get on that test tomorrow?" He stopped in his tracks, looked over his shoulder and did a little nod with his lower chin and said, "I don't know what you're thinking Aunt Cheri, but I am getting an "A" on that exam tomorrow." We both started laughing and off he went with his pajama bottoms and oversized shoes. I told myself he is one fast learner!!

A couple days later, I called to find out the results of the Science Final Exam. He was so happy he could barely control his excitement. He said. "Aunt Cheri I took your advice and not only did I receive an "A" on my final exam but my Rocket Ship went the farthest!"

I congratulated him and I told him that anything is possible if you have the mindset, ***will*** and desire to achieve!

Table of Contents

1. The Child Inside

Playing in the backyard, taking a bike ride, swimming in the pool or perhaps making angels in the snow; all of these examples illustrate how simple life was as a child. There were no worries, fears or concerns, except maybe when our next meal was being served or our next play date.

The innocence of a child compels us to look, reflect and see the world through their eyes. Whether it's the vibrant colors of the rainbow, the scent of blooming flowers or the anticipation of their favorite treat, each of these instances symbolizes life and its simplicity. However, as we move through the years, we complicate it by placing rules and conditions which lead us to define ourselves by what we do and what we have.

When did the simplicity of these daily experiences disappear for us? Are we so caught up in our day to day tasks that we forget to live in the moment? How often have you listened to the rain as it softly cascades down your window or the soft touch of the grass blades as your toes engulf the richness of nature? These are the moments we need to capture and embrace. The beauty of our surroundings is captivating and the benefit it can provide can be stimulating and add fuel to your fire.

As a child, there was never a "To Do" list or items that needed to be completed before we turned in for the evening. Our little minds could not comprehend stress or feeling depressed. We could always dream big and think without limitations. I remember as a young child in school, the teacher would go around the classroom and ask you "What do you want to be when you grow up?" You would hear an astronaut, the president, a police officer or a doctor. The answers were given freely and without constraints. We were not only convinced but believed we could become whatever we dreamed!

How empowering it must have felt, knowing we had the support of our teachers, parents, and siblings guiding us towards our goals and dreams. We trusted they had our best interest at hand and would support us through our successes and failures.

A Child's Progression

The simple tasks of tying your shoes for the first time, learning the alphabet or counting to 50, were monumental successes as a child and gave us the confidence we needed to keep moving forward. It reinforced some basic fundamentals that if we work hard we can accomplish the task at hand.

As we developed through our teenage years, our concerns and priorities changed but we still felt we could reach for the stars. Our anxiety now comes from missing the bus, picking out the right outfit for school or sitting at the “cool” lunch table with all the popular kids. Simple, yet so complicated in the eyes of a teenager.

For many years, I would attend my nephew’s track meets and cross country events and their enthusiasm and excitement was palpable. You could feel their anticipation as they approached the starting line, waiting for the gun to sound, indicating the start of the race. Their only concern in that moment was to get to the finish line as quickly as possible. No worries. They were in the moment and nothing else mattered.

As they progressed through high school more alarms were sounding. What events will I participate in? Am I bystander or participant? Their sphere of influence is now growing from new friendships, school activities or committees. As adults we try to instill good morals and values that will guide and motivate them to make sound decisions in the future.

Then as high school draws to a close, they're off to college. Their high school friends are being disbursed to different colleges and new friendships will develop. Where did the time ago? My baby is going away. But he/she is not a baby any longer. They have matured, gained their independence and a new path in their life is being shaped. They will grow in self-awareness and understand the aspects of their personal growth and development.

Pivotal Point

They now hit a pivotal point in their life filled with exciting and new experiences. Free from the constraints of their parents and new found freedom. Strain and anxiety build up from daily homework, tuition bills and pass / fail grades.

As the years progress, worry and doubt start to creep in. They begin questioning themselves and their ability. Is this even possible? Can I really accomplish my dreams? However, a few years ago when they graduated from high school, their dreams were within their reach.

In such a short time, their minds become clouded. What causes us to question our potential? Are we being influenced by friends, professors or perhaps our environment?

It saddens me that we become tainted by our surroundings, social media, the internet, news media and family members who question our thought processes and cause us to think our dreams are a distant memory.

Rest assured, I am not placing everyone under this umbrella of self-doubt. But I dare you to sit back and contemplate your life. Is there something you have always dreamed about but never took that leap of faith for fear of failure?

Has Your Dream Disappeared?

Where was the foundation we built as a child and declared we could become anything we dreamed? Life can be difficult as we mature into adults and some of our dreams have been placed on the sidelines until further notice.

Are you familiar with any of these excuses?

- I'll start my business when ALL the bills are paid
- When the kids are out of the house
- I need to save $5,000 first
- After I pay for the kid's college

Do some of these resonate with you? Friends, I am here to tell you, there will never be a right time. The time is now!

If you have a passion or dream tucked away, start today by taking baby steps. Yes, take off the training wheels, get rid of the excuses; it's time to step out of your comfort zone and move forward.

I am not saying it's going to be easy and yes, it will be uncomfortable. You need to ignite the passion inside. Stir it up, keep the dream alive. It's a choice.

Create that "To Do" list but create it for you and YOUR DREAM! You will be amazed at what you can accomplish in one year by doing the little things that all add up to your ultimate goal.

Your passion and dream is what should motivate you and keep you focused throughout the day.

Has your dream disappeared? Are you ready to make a change? Then let's begin!

"Go confidently in the direction of your dreams. Live the life you've imagined."

~Henry David Thoreau

2. Are You At Your Peak?

You're sitting back in your lazy boy deciding should I turn on the TV, get a bowl of ice cream or read that good novel I recently purchased. Another day has come and gone and our goal is to sit back, relax and enjoy the evening. I understand and we have all been there.

Had a rough day at the office where the boss was yelling all day about deadlines and your kids are pulling and tugging at you about everything from homework assignments, attending school activities or play dates with their friends.

Let me ask you something - Why aren't you contemplating the business you should be opening, or going back to college to become that accountant you have always dreamed about or perhaps opening up an art gallery to display your paintings. You wouldn't be reading this book unless you were considering a career change – right?

What is preventing you from moving forward? You know the seed is there, it's always been there, but for some reason there was always an excuse preventing you from executing your true passion. It's a desire, a burning passion knowing you have more to accomplish. When you think about your passion, there is excitement and enthusiasm. But how will I get there? Who will listen to me? How much time will it take? And finally, what will my family think?

Those burning questions automatically start creating a fear factor and *fear* is the number ONE emotion that holds us back.

Can I Do It?

I love Henry Ford's famous quote:

If You Think You Can Do A Thing
Or
Think You Can't Do A Thing – Your Right!

Every day we make thousands of decisions, both major and minor ones. Whether to eat that decadent chocolate cake, brush our teeth or change careers. With each of our choices, there are real life consequences and our path in life is based upon the choices we have made: good or bad.

Begin by moving forward. There is nothing you can do to change the past. The past is just a given point in time where you can glance through the window learn from your mistakes and celebrate your victories.

Folding is NOT An Option

Do you realize you have total control over whom you socialize with, what you do, where you work and how you think and deal with difficulties. I know what you're thinking; You have no idea what I am going through or the type of hand I have been dealt. No, I do not know what kind of hand the game of life has sent your way, but I do know you can't win by folding.

We all know if you have four aces in your hand, the chances of winning is pretty darn good but what if you are dealt a pair of deuces? Are you going to render yourself powerless and fold because you were anticipating something else?

Quit believing the hand you have been dealt is flawed. Learn to play your hand well and succeed despite your circumstances. Sometimes you need to take chances in life to change your situation.

You Have More To Accomplish

The joy and happiness we desire is based upon our attitude. I have always felt your altitude is a direct reflection of your attitude. How do you see your glass? Is it half empty or half full?

Just because you were born on the other side of tracks does not mean you have to settle for second best. I have a perfect example to illustrate this point and it's very near and dear to my heart and involves my older sister.

My sister and her husband always had a dream to move to Florida and open up a Hyperbaric Chamber Center. Based on her circumstances at the time, a normal person would think this was only a pipe dream.

First of all, they were in their mid-twenties, she was working as Human Resource Manager for a paint distribution center, barely paying their bills, raising two young babies and her husband had yet to get accepted to Medical School.

Now, that my friend, are a lot of odds playing against you. In fact, my brother-in-law had to apply two separate times to get accepted into MSU's Medical Program. The school only allows you to apply once a year and they only select a finite number of students into their program.

On his second attempt, he did get accepted but in spite of the great news, the hard times would begin. He goes off to Medical School while my sister works full time trying to raise two young children. This was a very difficult time for her. She was trying to support a husband and be a single mom to her children.

Eight years later my brother-in-law graduates from Medical School and receives the Cum Laude recognition for outstanding grades.

Their dream now appears to be closer, maybe just a flicker but there is light. The residency training has been completed, he is now a Neurologist and their decision to move to Florida has been decided. They have finalized their plans, made some contacts and their travel destination is Key West, Florida where he will begin practicing medicine.

The day they left was a host of mixed emotions. Happy their dreams were now a reality and sad they were moving away.

Happy Ending

Their story does have a final chapter and a very happy ending. My sister and her husband opened up the first private Hyperbaric Chamber Center in the United States back in 1997. It has been very successful over the years and my sister officially retired at the ripe age of 52.

But she did not stop there. She pursued her culinary degree and graduated Summa Cum Laude and today volunteers her culinary expertise, free of charge, to the Woman's shelter in Florida. She understands giving back is an important way of expressing kindness and gratitude for all that has been given to her.

They continue to make residual money on the Hyperbaric Chamber and my brother-in-law now gives lectures around the world.

Anything is possible if you believe in yourself. It's now your turn to step out in faith and fulfill your dreams. Quit letting those negative voices prevent you from pursuing something you have always dreamed about.

"The future belongs to those who believe in the beauty of their dreams"
~Eleanor Roosevelt

3. Let's Do This Together

You have 100 ideas swirling around your head, there is no direction and your thoughts seem to be coming and going like a revolving door. It all seems so overwhelming and you're wondering, where do I begin? Your natural impulse is to do nothing. Days and weeks go by and still nothing has been accomplished and you continue to struggle. Believe me when I say this, we have all been there before. What you need to do, is break down the tasks into manageable portions. Now just sit back, take a deep breath and let's do this together.

Make a Plan

Sometime the hardest thing is to take that step of faith and start making a plan. Your plan should outline the steps you need to take in order to reach your goal. The most important thing is to stay organized and document your success.

Start your first page with a heading entitled "Goals." It seems pretty basic but more often than not, when you write them down in black and white they appear real. Make sure your goals are attainable. Your goals should make you feel a little uncomfortable but not unreachable.

When outlining your goals use the acronym SMART. If you're not familiar with this acronym it stands for specific, measurable, acceptable, realistic and timely. These descriptive words will keep you moving forward as you plan your life's passion and dreams.

Start with page two and label this "Objectives." Your goals were focused around the big picture and your objectives will be more specific. If your goal is to create a new company, your first step is: Start investigating your local state website and begin printing out the appropriate corporate documents. The second step is: Complete the forms and mail them back to the appropriate person. The third would be: Obtain an Employee Identification Number(EIN) number from the IRS. (Your EIN is your company's social security number and it is obtained online through the IRS). Now you are on a roll, and every time you complete a task, you will feel a sense of accomplishment.

Your objectives should be precise and can be checked off as you complete them. As you continue to work your plan and alter your goals, there is a very strong possibility you will encounter several hills and valleys. However, remember to keep pushing forward and don't take your eye off the prize. Sometimes these road blocks are very frustrating and could prevent you from fulfilling your dreams, other times they are placed in your path to make you grow beyond your normal boundaries. There were many days I wanted to throw in the towel and get a "real job" with a real pay check, but I knew if I kept my focus on the end result, I would obtain my dream. I also realized, if it was so easy to be a business owner then everyone would be doing it. Right!

My Business Opportunity

When I opened up my first business back in 2002, I knew absolutely nothing about being an entrepreneur. My background included being a Respiratory Therapist for 10 years and then I decided to go back to school to become a Computer Science Major. As life would have it, I lost my job in June of 2002. The company I was working for was bought by General Electric and most of us were unemployed within 3 months. I was given severance pay and bonuses which was contingent on transferring all the company's data to India. During this time, I tried effortlessly to find a job but during 2002 the economy was struggling and no one was hiring.

While visiting my sister in California, (a trip that was booked prior to losing my job) she approached me about a business opportunity. On the last day of our visit, she gave me some documents and encouraged me to look into this industry. I really had nothing to lose since I was currently unemployed. When I arrived home I worked non-stop for seven straight days, reading, researching, studying and investigating everything about this business. My husband changed one of our bedrooms into an office which consisted of a computer, printer/fax machine and a phone. On the eighth day I began making "code calls." Anyone with a sales background knows it's NOT "code calls" its "Cold Calls." You see, I knew nothing about opening a business let alone making a sales call.

However, before I went to bed each evening, I created a spreadsheet of 50 people I would call the following day. This went on for 6 straight months. My first order came through in about 45 days and like they say, the rest is history. It became successful, and I have opened up several businesses since then.

The business that started everything for me was a Mobile Notary business. This business involved contracting a notary to close a set of mortgage documents anywhere in the United States. I had a large database of notaries who did this for a living. I would negotiate a price with the Title Company and negotiate a price with notary and the difference between these two fees would be my profit.

My story helps to illustrate faith, consistency, perseverance, commitment, determination and dedication. I created my call list every day, faithfully. I made those phone calls consistently every day, without fail. I have to admit, the first week of cold calling was very unnerving. I had people hanging up on me continuously, but in the back of my mind, I knew there were people who needed what I had to offer, they just didn't know it yet! This motto kept me going each day! Yes, it can be trying on your nerves, but I knew I wanted to be successful and kept pushing myself forward each day.

Make Progress

Are you doing something each day to meet your goals and objectives or are you always busy being busy? You have to discipline yourself in order to stay on track. If your goal is worth achieving, then it's worth completing. To reach your goals, you need to take action each day, each week and each month. If you create the list, there is a sequence of events that will unfold to produce the desired results.

It's almost impossible to anticipate everything you will need to accomplish. Although, the benefit of having a plan, is that it allows you to be flexible and make course corrections without deviating too far from your route.

As you progress, I guarantee you will need to make some minor adjustments but make sure your changes keep you focused and heading towards your target.

Don't allow distractions to keep you from being laser focused. Here are some helpful tips to keep you moving forward:

1) Have Well Defined Goals
2) Your Objectives Are Your Action Items
3) Prioritize Your List
4) Track Your Progress
5) Plan Ahead
6) Reward Yourself For Your Successes
7) Remove Distractions
8) Block Out Time
9) Keep Focused On Your Target
10) Ask For Help!

These 10 techniques can be applied in your personal life, as well as, your professional life. By implementing these basic steps, it will keep you on track and maximize your success.

"Visualize this thing you want. See it, feel it, believe in it. Make your mental blueprint and begin"
~ Robert Collier

4. Create Space

It's the age old question we face each day. There just aren't enough hours in the day. Now the last time I checked, I believe everyone had the same amount of hours, 24 to be exact. Then why is it that some people can manage their time. They get so much more accomplished and still have time for family, work and friends. Do they have better time management skills?

Yes, I believe time management plays a role but the other half is about managing your energy. What is it you *"Want Out Of Life?"* In order to get what you want, you have to take the time for the people and things that mean the most to you.

Set An Intention

Each morning set your intention and stay focused on your results. Your intention could be creating your "To Do" list or perhaps making on important phone call. Whatever it is, place emphasis on the task throughout your day and you will be less likely to get sidetracked.

Setting your intention demonstrates a commitment to achieving your desired results. It means you need to take action. Nothing will come to you by sitting on the couch, hoping something or someone will show up. Where you are right now is based upon what you believe. What You Believe – You Achieve! There are no accidents.

When your intention is set, you feel inspired to move forward. This motivation comes from a place of passion. Always follow your instincts, putting action behind your intention. Moving forward, you will have greater control of how you spend your time; everyone's goal is to work smarter, not harder.

Relax and Have Fun

Give yourself time to have fun and be creative. I think that as adults, we forget the playful side of life. Rekindle the playful part of YOU! When was the last time you blew bubbles or flew a kite? When we allow ourselves to let our right brain take over, the problems we were trying to solve suddenly appear obvious to us. Was that a coincidence?

Some of us have placed our life on auto-pilot and go throughout each day doing the same methodical routine. Our logical, analytical left brain kicks in and your list involves getting the kids off to school, getting to work, attending school activities, making dinner, doing homework, getting ready for the next day, only to repeat ALL these steps the very next day.

Create more time in your life by learning to say "No." There are many ways to say no and still do it with love and joy in your heart. The next time you are approached, try saying "That just doesn't work for me, right now." If you begin to implement this statement, you will embrace your new found freedom and the autonomy it can create.

It's impossible to be everything for everybody and if you're going to try, you will end up feeling defeated and irritable. It's important to value who you are and what you want first. Take time for you and your family before you agree to "Yes."

Too Busy

Let's begin to address this *time* issue. Time is all around you, you just haven't recognized those moments when the gift is available to you. The next time you are caught in traffic, give gratitude for this quiet time in the car, instead of cursing out the accident or person holding up traffic. We have all been in those predicaments, use this time to reflect or be creative. When you're home alone for a short time, instead of turning on the TV or CD, use this time as a gift, enjoy it and be productive.

I know you're a little confused, since your definition of time may be something completely different. The difference is, it did not come in a nice neat package as you had imagined. You see when you look at your activities throughout the day, there are plenty of moments when you do have time. Stay in the moment and do not ignore those instances, you will never get this *time* back.

I find my best time to be creative is in the morning getting ready for work. It may be only 15 to 30 minutes but my ideas are manifested first thing in the morning, after I have slept. It's not to say I don't have creative ideas throughout the day, but my discernment and subconscious seem to work overtime in the morning. I take advantage of this quiet time and I always have a pen and pad ready to write down my next earth shattering revelation!

Recognize Your Successes

C'mon were in a hurry, get your brother, we're late. How many times have these similar phrases been echoed? Were so busy; being busy, we forget to recognize our successes along the way.

How about the warm hug from your child this morning, the confirmation from a new client or the accomplishment of running 1 mile. These events and circumstances are all successes but we cast them aside as everyday events. Enjoy these moments and recognize your achievements and accomplishments.

The mere fact of bringing a human life into this world, is a priceless gift of love. Obtaining a new client is a huge achievement in this competitive work force and running a mile is a milestone in anyone's life and should be applauded as a job well done!

Vision Board

Have you ever experienced the power of a vision board? A vision board is a series of pictures and words which constantly remind you of your goals.

It is a powerful tool that inspires you to take action so you never lose sight of your dreams. Keep in mind this vision board is for You and about You.

Make yourself accountable by sharing your dreams with family and friends. When you begin discussing your future goals, your vision board should come into full view. Your dreams now become part of your reality and you are being held accountable by communicating those desires.

This vision board should also identify what you want, what you believe and the confidence to meet those objectives. Finally, you need to have conviction. You have to believe that you can achieve your heart's desire and you deserve to be rewarded.

Remember to reflect on this vision board (*Try Pinterest*) daily to explore new possibilities and create a life you love.

Growing Pains

There is no mistake; change can be difficult, but without it you will never grow to reach new heights. Growth only occurs when you move out of your comfort zone and start moving in a direction which makes you feel uncomfortable. Staying complacent and going through the same motions will only yield you the same results.

If you're looking for success, change is inevitable. Success is a combination of how you can positively impact the lives around you and leave a legacy others can emulate.

If you are not satisfied with your routine and are ready to make a change, it's time to take action. Don't be afraid to take a leap of faith and make the change you have been seeking.

"A year from now you will wish you had started today"
~ Karen Lamb

5. Putting the Pieces Together

Life can be one big puzzle. You have 100 pieces to the puzzle but how will they all fit together. Your mission, if you choose to accept it, is to gather all the pieces, separate them into different categories and begin shaping your puzzle. Your puzzle will be unique and will take on a shape and size based upon your goals and desires.

As you progress, you will see the puzzle reveal a beautiful landscape of opportunities, challenges, discoveries, victories and above all secrets about who you are.

We will never understand our full potential until we challenge ourselves to go beyond our limits. When we begin hiking up the mountain, it looks very steep and the peak appears unreachable.

Climbing life's mountain can be challenging, both physically and emotionally. Some of us will give up half way, and others will climb to the top. I want you to reach your peak! However, in order to get there, you need to gather your strength; have the endurance to face life's challenges and persevere.

Once you have achieved your first hurdle, take a look at the ***view***! Listen to the birds chirping a familiar melody or the wind whistling through the array of trees. The beauty and its splendor is a feeling, like a piece of art. Enjoy its splendor. You have achieved a milestone, Congratulations!

Okay, back to business. You have taken time out to recognize your achievements. This is a key element to your success. If you don't stop to acknowledge these victories, you will become disappointed and frustrated.

Keep in mind, there will always be another peak or valley waiting on the sidelines, but try and stay on the winning side. Tackle it one day at a time and keep prioritizing your tasks. See where you can combine tasks to maximize your time.

Making The Cut

Over the years, through our failures and victories, we have gained a wealth of knowledge and wisdom. I am a firm believer there are no coincidences. Every failure or accident has a silver lining. Our job is to evaluate the circumstances and look for the opportunity.

I have a personal example where I had to decide, if I would "*Make the Cut.*" I was an owner of a Title Company when the real estate crash occurred in

2008. My business decreased by 75% literally, overnight. I went from 15 employees down to one. Homes were being foreclosed, house values were declining at an alarming rate, consumers were losing their jobs and no one was buying or purchasing homes. My entire business and livelihood was dependent on closing real estate transactions and I was not prepared for the fall out.

Unfortunately, the one thing I failed to consider in my planning phase was the economy and the state of affairs of our government. How could I have predicted this calamity? Yes, there were signs and economists were alluding to such a catastrophe. Could consumers afford their house payment once their interest rate readjusted? I guess we all know the answer to this question.

This Too Shall Pass

As I reflect back and review the series of events, it made me realize we will always encounter trials that are out of our control. I believe that true achievers don't succumb to their environment, they create their own opportunities.
Are you wondering whether or not I "Made the Cut?" The answer is YES! There was a lot of soul searching during this phase in my life but I was able

to see the silver living. Those events which seemingly looked like a catastrophe were truly an awakening. "As a man thinketh in his heart so is he" Proverbs 23:7

How you think about a situation is what you will become. Believe you are destined to live a life of excellence. Yes, we all have a unique set of circumstances we need to overcome, but do not let those events dictate your future. You have all the power to create your own destiny. Think positive, be encouraged and let go of limitations. You are a victor, you are talented and you will become what you believe. Believe every day you are destined to achieve your goals and dreams.

Lessons Learned

The number one lesson I learned during this period was to never be complacent! Keep learning, keep searching and above all keep smiling.

Your customer base will change and evolve over time, but your goal is to create solid relationships and exceptional customer service. Many business owners lose sight of their customers and become focused on the bottom line. This diversion causes customer attrition, and over time, it will create a loss of business leading to a decrease in revenue.

For most business owners this can be a balancing act. You tip the scale too far to the right you lose profit and too far to the left and you lose customers. There is really no easy solution but if you maintain customer loyalty and anticipate their needs, you will have a customer for life.

Pareto's Principle

A simple rule to follow in your personal or professional life is Pareto's Principle which is the 80/20 rule. This rule implies 20% of the activity you work on, accounts for 80% of your productivity.

If you always keep this ratio in the back of your mind, then you will always be prepared and focus on the important things that need to be accomplished and "work smarter" instead of working harder.

We all become sidetracked with distractions. One minute we're researching information on the internet and the next moment we' re on Facebook and two hours have elapsed. Sound familiar?
To help minimize some of those distractions, here are a few suggestions:

- Create a daily schedule
- Let your phone calls go to voicemail and then return them all at once
- Have a set time to read and respond to emails
- Set your working hours
- Find an accountability partner
- Split task's into manageable sub-tasks.
- Turn off alerts from incoming mail or social networking sites.
- Create a "To Do" list
- Allow for quiet time
- Complete everything you start
- Organize and prioritize your tasks each day
- Schedule breaks
- Create obtainable goals
- Delegate
- Declutter your desk

Your goal is to stay focused and begin today by finding fulfillment and living by this 80/20 rule.

New Beginnings

Isn't it great to wake up and know you have another day to make it right? Don't delay another minute, it's time. Erase all those errors and wipe the chalkboard clean. With a clean slate in front you, write down your ambitions and desires.

C'mon don't cheat and start looking in your rear view mirror. There is nothing you can do to change your past, keep looking forward and make your future brighter and more alive. Take everything you have learned through your failures and successes and make each day a *New Beginning*.

The person you are today is based upon the choices you made and with every choice; good or bad, there are consequences. Therefore, use the wisdom and knowledge you have gained throughout life to make sound decisions which are in align with your goals.

"Every story has an ending. But in life, every ending is a new beginning "
~Unknown

6. Ask For Help

It's impossible to know all the answers and sometimes it can be difficult to ask for help. Some of us have this internal drive to do everything ourselves. "No one could ever do it as good as me." Sound familiar?

However, we could spend endless hours being frustrated and confused. Asking for help does not show a sign of weakness, rather it allows others to share their knowledge and expand our learning curve. Leave behind those feelings of embarrassment and humble yourself to ask for help. Being able to ask for help, is a key element in reaching your peak.

Personally, I have the tendency to be the "Lone Ranger," but through the years, I fully understood there is a balance between asking for help and performing the task myself. I find it's so much easier to offer my services and help others, than it is to ask for help.

Asking for help; brings out the vulnerability issue. It exposes us to areas we are not comfortable with. We all have insecurities and weaknesses but there are endless resources available to help us break down the barrier. Asking for assistance is vital to your growth and development.

Set The Pace

Sometimes the answers are not always readily available. It may take several phones calls or multiple resources in order to come up with the solution.

This takes me back to a time when it took me over a week to make the right contact. Years ago when I was trying to obtain my Title Insurance Producer's license, there was a *little* requirement I needed to meet in order to obtain this license. (I use *little* facetiously because this *little* requirement was one BIG issue).

I searched for weeks trying to find a class, outline or person who could help meet this prerequisite. I made over 50 phone calls and each person was constantly pointing me in a new direction. It felt like I was going in circles many days and each morning I would start the entire process over. After about 7 days, I finally reached a person who could answer my question. After a long conversation, it turned out the State I reside in; did not have any classes or outlines I could follow.

The only thing she suggested was that I purchase the seven Law Insurance books and study those volumes. *Really.* I honestly thought she was joking and suddenly realized she was being serious.

After my stomach rebounded and it was out of my throat, I said "Why Not?" I have this tenacious, type A personality where I believe I am "Super Women" and why couldn't I achieve this overwhelming, unassuming task?

Much to my surprise, I bought the seven Insurance Law books and started studying for something I had no idea what I was studying for. I created flash cards, started memorizing case studies and then one day I decided I was ready for the BIG day.

I drove down to the state capital at 8:00 am and the exam started at 9:00 am. I was a little nervous, but knew I had spent hours studying and was determined to pass the test. I began reading the questions very slowly and suddenly an alarm starting going off – HELP – I don't know the answer to any of these questions.

Suddenly I am panic stricken and started hyperventilating. I am telling myself to calm down, everything will be okay, this is only a test. (The same phrase you hear when they're testing the emergency system on your TV) Yes, but I need to pass this test in order to obtain my license. This was going to be my livelihood, my new career, my life, but this exam turned out to be one of the longest hours of my life. In fact, it seemed like I would never get to question 100.

Between feeling disappointed and wanting to leave this entire experience behind me, I had to pick myself up and *walk the plank* to hand in my exam. My Scantron form would be scanned and within seconds my results, my life, would be revealed.

Did I Pass or Fail, Pass or Fail. The anticipation was rocking my world but deep down I knew the answer. I had FAILED, and the lady clearly seen my disappointment and said, "You can take the test again in 24 hours." Wow, what a great conciliation, since I barely knew the answer to any of the questions. Obviously, I had studied all the wrong material and in that moment I was only focusing on one thing and it involved trying to memorize some of the exam questions, so I could begin studying the right topics!

Finally, one fine day, I did pass the exam and I obtained my Title Insurance License. In spite of all the challenges, I never quit asking for help and found the answers I needed to achieve my goal. It was my perseverance, tenacity and the prize, my Title Insurance Producer License, which allowed me to keep moving forward.

What I learned throughout this experience is to set your own pace. Life is not a race but a marathon and take as much time as you need to complete the task. It may not always work out in your designated time frame but enjoy the journey and grow from each experience.

Every time I think about this incident I have to chuckle. I was convinced my life was defined around passing this one exam. As wisdom would have it, you realize this is just an instant of time and every life experience, including your successes and failures, defines who you are. We are here to make each experience count and find a balance between today's events and where you see yourself tomorrow.

Run Your Own Race

Is there really a finish line to your race? A lot us were taught at a young age, you have to work hard to accomplish your goals, which leads us to buy more, earn more and ultimately spend more.

Each day you wake up, your life revolves around choices. Will I argue with the boss today or will I perform my daily exercise? Whatever you decide will influence the outcome. There will always be another hill to climb, issue to resolve, or battle to fight.

The key to your growth is how we run the race. Are you always running trying to get to the end result? On your journey, did you evaluate your progress, analyze your problems, encounter obstacles and solve each one correctly? These are just questions to reflect and meditate on.

If we keep sprinting and forget about the journey, how will we ever understand the depth of the footprints we left behind? Each step we take leaves a unique footprint about our life and path. Life and all its fullness is a collection of memories and experiences which build upon themselves. Don't miss out on life's richest lessons. Experience the beauty of life through hardships and successes. It's through our hardships that we learn our biggest lessons.

Remember you are the only one who will write your final chapter. Make it unique. The decisions you make today will influence the direction you take in the future.

Let the rain wash away those footprints of limitations, uncertainties and fear. Move forward with confidence and *Run Your Own Race* making your path unique to you!

"The miracle isn't that I finished. The miracle is that I had the courage to start."
~ John Bingham

7. Winding Down

It's time to change directions. You have been going down the same path, doing the same thing and expecting different results. Your frustration level is reaching new heights, you want to make a change but that silent voice keeps telling you; "You will never accomplish your dreams."

Take the first step and start changing your thoughts. Sometimes taking the first step can be the most challenging, but the person who is destined to move ahead, trusts enough in their ability and takes that chance.

A lot can be learned from successful people like Abraham Lincoln and Bill Gates who persevered through some of the most challenging phases of their life. Each of them never gave up, plowed through the trenches and reached their mountain top.

It is never easy to stretch yourself and take a risk, especially when the next step feels like you're blindfolded. Some of us like to take the easy route and feel secure with our daily routine. We like to wrap our arms around the security we hold for ourselves, stay in the background and come home to those loving smiles of our loved one.

I know there are a lot of you that have great ideas and inventions, but you're just too afraid to take the risk. You know the worst part about being complacent, is that another person comes along, who is willing to take the chance, and they soar like an eagle using one of your ideas or discoveries.

Now you're frustrated and you have just watched another individual profit from your inspiration. For some of you, it will feel like defeat and for others it will be the motivating factor to seek out other opportunities. Remember life does not wait for anyone. If your heart is resonating and every beat is driving you to take a chance, don't look back, take the dive.

Nothing Ever Appears As It Seems

Most business entrepreneurs and owners have encountered many disappointments before they reached their peak. Their stories are inspiring and have always kept me motivated to keep pursuing my dream.

However, there are many individuals who only look at the end result and make remarks such as "They have all the luck," "They are always on the golf course," or "They have banker's hours." The problem with these remarks stems from the fact that; they clearly do not understand what it takes to keep a business afloat and moving forward on a daily basis. There is always the constant anxiety of keeping your customers satisfied or speculating if your top performers will work for your competitors or third, will there be enough revenue to meet payroll?

All of these concerns, plus a host of many more, are all legitimate concerns to business owners every day. For myself there were many days I had sleepless nights wondering how to manage all these tasks, still remain fair and keep my integrity?

The Shark Tank

When I started my business, I never realized the shark invested field I was about to encounter. I was the first business women in my area to open up a Title Insurance company. Before I ever opened my doors for business, I encountered two episodes from previous owners (Note: I said "previous") who wanted to make it perfectly clear I was not welcome in this industry.

One of the owners of a nearby Title company would repeatedly circle my office in an unmarked car every day for about month. He also tried to prevent me from obtaining an underwriter in my state which meant I could not open for business. My only recourse was to call the Vice President of this very large organization and tell them collusion was occurring. Before the phone call ended, I was able to underwrite for the entire state.

My other encounter occurred when I received a phone call from another Title company owner who wanted to meet me for lunch. I eagerly accepted. I thought, finally, someone in this industry wants to welcome me into their circle. Talk about being a green, naïve business owner. As you can imagine the luncheon did not go as I had anticipated. He began the conversation with, “Cheri you will never make it in this industry. I am giving you some sound advice and you need to consider coming to work for me. This is a male dominated field and you are going to sink.” Once I was over the shock of this proposition, I politely said thank you, but I am not interested. I plan on opening next week and walked out of the restaurant.

These challenging confrontations were one of the motivating factors that kept me moving towards my dream. There were several more issues which surfaced from these two gentlemen but I made a promise to myself, I would shine and succeed in spite of these obstacles, but underneath my breath I whispered, “May the best ***man*** win.”

Do You Believe In Karma?

Whether you believe it or not, Karma is always working in the background. The first gentlemen, who almost prevented me from opening my business, suffered a terrible illness, is bed ridden and no longer operates his business. The second gentlemen could no longer sustain his business and the company I merged with four years ago, bought out his firm. To make matters worse, he had to sit in my office and I became his manager.

I did not echo my concerns to dampen your spirit or discourage you, in fact, I wanted to ignite your inner spark and provide solid evidence anything is possible. This story was drawn from my own personal experience and proves dreams can be fulfilled through perseverance and determination.

Make no mistake, it takes nerves of steel to go outside your boundaries, but teflon nerves are not created when everything is coming up roses. They are shaped and molded during the most difficult moments of our life. Therefore, untie the strings, break free and let go of all limitations.

Tying The Pieces Together

Have you ever wondered if there's something you need to know, more to learn, more to experience or more to enjoy?

Life is full of opportunities. Just stop and look around. There are so many people who focus on their challenges and miss their opening. The amount of resources we have available today compared to five years ago is astounding. Tap into these sources and run your race. You need to look at every opportunity as your golden egg. Recognize these chances and use your knowledge and wisdom to improve your life.

However, many of you will not recognize the door being presented. The ideas or inspirations being manifested may be disguised in the form of a hardship. During an adversity it can be very difficult to see the silver lining, but begin by focusing on the positive and look for ways to overcome the obstacle or objection instead of giving up. This will boost your confidence and you will clearly see the advantage of the opportunity being presented.

There will never be the perfect time. Don't be the person sitting on the sidelines wishing and procrastinating. I want you to experience everything life has to offer. Spread your wings and begin flying like an eagle. Life is yours to experience!

"We are what we repeatedly do. Excellence then, is not an act, but a habit."
~ Aristotle

8. Bring About Change & Rejoice

It's your time. Are you prepared for the next chapter of your life? You have an incredible amount of information you have gained through your own personal experiences. Your story needs to be told. Whether it's opening a business, writing a book, becoming a famous artist or being an Olympic athlete, your path has the power to ignite and empower others. By giving them support and encouragement you can help them reach their potential. This action is known as the "domino effect." You see the benefit of empowering others is that your light will turn brighter as you ignite their internal flame.

Everyone needs encouragement. Life can be challenging and each of us can be overwhelmed by our circumstances. However, you can make a world of difference in someone's life by giving a small word of encouragement or perhaps a warm smile.

Keeping positive and passing this energy forward can improve outcomes, events and overall happiness in your life, as well as, the person you are mentoring. As you stay positive and align your thoughts towards your goals it will help you manifest your desires. Change your life by changing your mind!

Desires Fulfilled

Did you know people who are more optimistic believe they have the ability to achieve their goals? They believe a setback will have an exceedingly large comeback; like water under the bridge, they will overcome.

People who have less stress take more risks, believing good things will come their way. Having this type of belief system will create positive outcomes. Understand that a thought always precedes a manifestation. Before you ever have the desire, you first have to think it. If you remain in a constant state of anticipation, expecting your goal to be accomplished, you will see your dreams fulfilled.

I have a perfect testimonial when you change your belief and perceptions about a specific situation, no matter what obstacle appears in your path, your world can change right before your eyes.

A few years ago my husband and I were interested in purchasing a home about a ½ hour south from our current residence. I had been telling him for years, we will purchase a ***foreclosed house.*** I really had no reason to believe otherwise, the desire was placed in my heart and I knew it was an absolute.

Then one fine day, the perfect home went on the market. It was two doors down from my sister, how perfect! I could see my two nephews daily or every week. I am sure my enthusiasm was no match to there's but nonetheless, I could see them grow up and attend all their extracurricular activities.

The house was a "Short Sale" which meant it would take a while to negotiate but since we were in no hurry, we placed our first bid. Within about five days, we were told someone had out bid us which meant we would be back in the market looking for another home.

About eight months later, the house was back on the market. The buyers refused to wait for the long short sale process and decided to cancel their purchase agreement. At this time, we placed a second bid. Our excitement was rising, I called my sister and told her the good news.

Once again, we were notified, we were out bid for the second time. We both became discouraged and I am thinking this was just not meant to be.

Again, we were back in the market looking for another home.

Approximately nine months later, the second buyers refused to wait for the short sale process and purchased another home. You know what that meant, the house was back on the market for a third time! I am thinking I cannot believe my fate.

Now I can barely control my excitement. I told myself the third time is a charm! We have this locked in, we will place our bid a little higher and the deal is ours! Would you believe we were outbid for the ***THIRD*** time! When I called my husband and told him what had happened, he was speechless. You could have heard a pin drop.

I called my sister and broke the news to her and the family. We were all very disappointed, except for my nephew, William, who was 12 years old at the time.

Do You Believe In Miracles?

One summer evening we were driving in the truck with both of my nephews in the back seat. William asked me to explain to him why we would not be moving down his street. I tried to put it into very simplistic terms and after I finished explaining, he looked at me and said, "Aunt Cheri, is there a possibility the people who are buying this house may not get the financing and it will go back on the market?" I told William, the chances are very slim but I guess anything is possible if you believe, and we ended our conversation.

Hold on to your shorts, because what I am about to tell you will make you think just a little different the next time you begin to have doubt or fear. Yes, the house went back on the market for the 4Th time! The buyers could not get financing, just like William had said! The house was up for sale but this time it was listed by the bank, because the house had gone through the foreclosure process.

It's now been 2 ½ years since I placed my first offer on this home. I had never been so nervous in all my life when I placed the fourth bid on ***my foreclosed house***. Now, what are the chances of getting another opportunity to bid on a home for the fourth time? Maybe a million to 1? I am not sure what the odds are but I am guessing it's pretty darn high. I am sure you are wondering what happened the fourth time around? YES, I WON THE BID!!! When I found out they accepted our offer, I was jumping up and down in my office, I was crying, I was laughing and completely shocked!

This one event has left an indelible mark on my heart. December 14th will mark our fourth anniversary of moving in our wonderful home. Every day I thank God for his faithfulness and goodness in my life.

My personal experience illustrates how unpredictable life can be. Yes, planning, saving and strategizing is important, but with the knowledge and experience I have gained, I now realize anything is possible. The shift was in my mindset. "The Impossible" is something we reiterate over and over again because we have not trained our minds or hearts to see past which does not yet exist.

In order to start living the "good life" you must start training your mind and heart beginning today. Turn the impossible into tomorrow's possibility. Create a state of mind expectancy, expecting your goal or dream to be accomplished and seeing no other options. Do not become a victim of your circumstance, work every day to create a positive outcome.

You know you're ready for a change when you are not satisfied with your daily routine. There is a knowing inside, you were meant to do something more with your life. It's time. Don't be afraid to take a leap of faith and make the change you have been seeking. Aristotle said, "You become what you do" It's time to quit observing from the sidelines and start living *your* dream.

The Final Chapter

How will you define your final chapter? Will you keep working just to have enough? How long will you feel frustrated before you make a change? Will someone always dictate what days you can take off or what time to punch in?

I have been an entrepreneur for over 13 years and I have never regretted one moment. Yes, it can be difficult and some days can be very challenging, but if you have the passion and determination to make a difference, then it's time to change your future. You see that when you decide to take the leap and begin pursuing your passion, it never feels like work. You get up every day with a sense of excitement wondering what opportunity lies ahead.

Begin using your imagination and wisdom and start manifesting your ideas and vision. Your strengths will always shine when you move in the direction of your greatest potential. S*hine* in your own brilliance.

"When Opportunity Knocks" did you walk through the door where your future is unwritten or will fear prevent you from opening the door? The choice is yours.

"New beginnings are often disguised as painful endings"
~ Anonymous

Epilogue

My gift was to encourage, motivate, empower and inspire you to reach your goals. Change is never easy. It's an internal battle we fight each day. Do we hold on to old habits or will we fight to let go? Release the hold and allow your fears to be lifted and carried away.

I believe that each of us has a purpose, a role in this world that needs to be fulfilled. The power is in your hands. Make a legacy with your steps and embrace change with an open heart and an open mind. Time will not stand still. Leave all those negative voices you hear at the door and begin performing those tasks which draw you closer to your passion and dream.

Final Thoughts

As I reflect back on this gift, this story, I am reminded that a book is really a mirror image. An image of someone's struggles and victories and how their fight inspired others to pursue their dreams. Something powerful occurs once we allow others to see inside our world.

This manuscript began as an inspirational book and ended up being a story of my life, Cheri Schultz!

Recommended Reading

Inspirational Quotes For Challenging Times
~ *Cheryl Schultz*

How to Win Friends & Influence People
~ *Dale Carnegie*

Fulfilling Your Soul's Potential
~ *Michael Beckwith*

The Greatest Networker in the World
~ *John Milton*

The Success Principles
~ *Jack Canfield*

Kick Your Excuses Goodbye
~ *Rene Godefroy*

Beach Money
~ *Jordan Adler*

Crush It
~ *Gary Vaynerchuk*

Law of Attraction
~ *Michael J. Losier*

The Last Lecture
~ *Randy Pausch*

Awakening To Your Life's Purpose
~ *Eckhart Tolle*

A Simple Path
~ *Mother Teresa*

Your Best Life Now
~ *Joel Osteen*

Change Your Thoughts - Change Your Life
~ *Dr. Wayne Dyer*

From the Heart: Seven Rules to Live By
~ *Robin Roberts*

"Ignite Your Light"

Don't Allow Your Past Heartaches to Define Your Future!

Discover techniques and methods to reduce your stress, unleash your potential and free yourself from self-sabotaging behaviors.

http://www.cherischultz.com

Inspirational Quotes For Challenging Times

This book is a collection of 70 original Inspirational Quotes (with Images) which inspired me during my difficulties. I am sharing these quotes in hopes they will encourage you to live for today knowing your tomorrows will get better. We all face challenges every day but with every obstacle there is always growth. I want to encourage you to enlarge your vision and stay positive in your thoughts. Enjoy and never stop reaching for your rainbow!

ASIN: B00GMWJS7Q
Kindle / 107 Pages
US $2.99

Made in USA
Fenton, MI
3 October 2016

Made in the USA
Monee, IL
27 September 2021